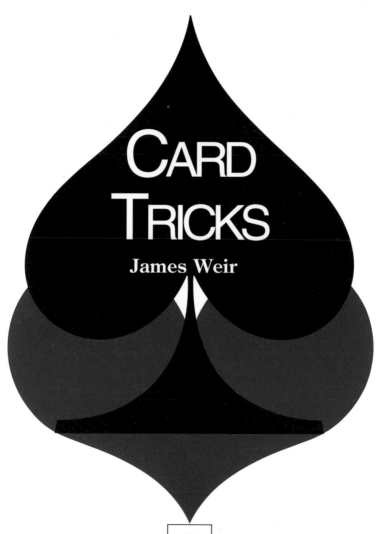

CARD TRICKS

James Weir

This is a Parragon Book
This edition published in 2001

Parragon
Queen Street House
4 Queen Street
Bath BA1 1HE, UK

ISBN: 0-75256-320-3

Produced by Haldane Mason, London

Printed in China

CONTENTS

♦ ♣ ♥ ♠ ♥ ♠ ♦ ♣ ♥ ♠ ♦ ♣ ♥ ♠ ♦ ♣

INTRODUCTION

All the tricks in this book are easy to learn and simple to perform. Even so, a little time spent in rehearsal will enhance their impact and improve your reputation as a performer.

So how much practice does a card trick need? Enough to ensure you perform it smoothly and can handle the cards with confidence. No one believes in a performer who is nervous, or who is not in control of the material. Practise until a trick becomes second nature, and you will give your presentation the polish these fine tricks deserve.

It is also a good idea to memorize the two golden rules of magical performance. Rule One: Never do the same trick twice for the same audience, no matter how hard they plead with you. Rule Two: Never bore your audience. Stop performing while they are still keen to see more. That way, you will be asked to entertain them another time.

Above all else, enjoy your magic. Card tricks are designed to divert and entertain, and there is no reason why you shouldn't enjoy each performance as much as your audience does.

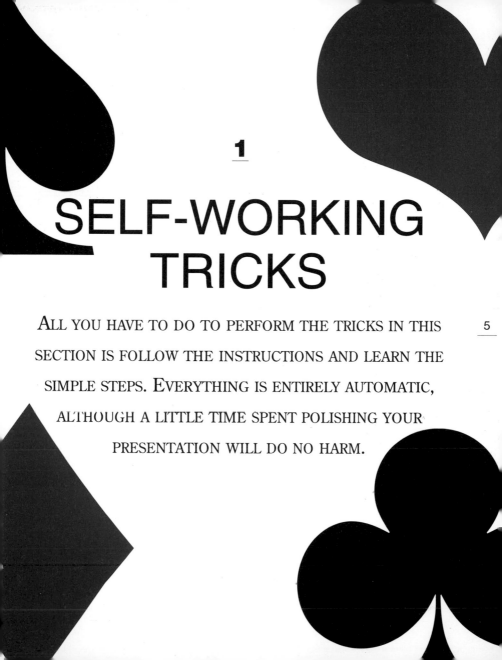

1

SELF-WORKING TRICKS

ALL YOU HAVE TO DO TO PERFORM THE TRICKS IN THIS SECTION IS FOLLOW THE INSTRUCTIONS AND LEARN THE SIMPLE STEPS. EVERYTHING IS ENTIRELY AUTOMATIC, ALTHOUGH A LITTLE TIME SPENT POLISHING YOUR PRESENTATION WILL DO NO HARM.

DO AS I DO

THE EFFECT

Performer and spectator have a pack of cards each, which they shuffle. Each then makes a selection from his own pack. Astonishingly, they choose identical cards.

THE METHOD

Use a red-backed and a blue-backed pack, so they can be easily distinguished. Give one pack to a spectator, saying, 'Whatever I do, you do the same.'

6

The packs are shuffled and cut, then you hand yours to the spectator and you take theirs. Shuffle as before, then exchange packs again, returning the spectator's pack face down; do this by holding the pack with your fingers at one end, thumb at the other, and move it past your line of vision as you lay it down.

As you glimpse the bottom card (e.g. the Four of Diamonds), remember it **(Fig. 1)**.

'Do as I do...' you say. Then spread your own pack in a ribbon,

1

2

lift a card from the middle of the spread and look at it **(Fig. 2)**.

Now say, 'Take a card and remember it.' In fact you simply go through the motions. There is no need to remember your card.

Next, square the face-down pack and put the chosen card on top, face down. The spectator does the same. Now make a complete cut, burying the chosen card.

'Give me your pack again, and you take mine.'

Swap packs and tell the spectator to take from your pack the card he looked at and put it face down on

the table – 'And I'll take mine from your pack.'

Spread the cards, faces towards you, looking for the remembered Four of Diamonds. When you find it, the card underneath will be the spectator's chosen card. Remove it and put it face down in front of you **(Fig. 3)**.

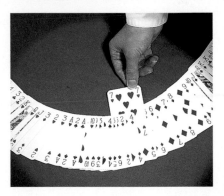

3

'Show us your card,' You say.

The spectator turns over his card. You pause, then turn your card. They are both the same.

'Well,' you say, 'you certainly did as I did.'

TURN-OVER CARD MYSTERY

THE EFFECT

A spectator takes a card from the pack and remembers it. It is put back, and when the pack is spread, the chosen card has turned face up.

THE METHOD

Before you begin, turn the bottom card of the face-down pack face up. When you spread the cards (Fig. 1), make sure the bottom card doesn't show.

1

Ask the spectator to take a card, then square the pack in your left hand and tell him or her to let others see it. 'Tonight, I'll allow witnesses,' you say.

As the card is shown around, your left hand drops casually to your side; on the way down, let the pack turn over in your hand. Do not rush this.

When you bring the hand up again, you are holding a squared-up pack with one face-down card on top. The rest are face up.

2

Take the chosen card from the spectator, keeping it face down, and push it very deliberately into the pack **(Fig. 2)**. Square up the cards.

'If I were a beginner at this,' you say, 'I'd try to find your card like this...'

Put the pack behind your back and look worried, like someone hopelessly fumbling for a card. In fact, you turn the top card over to face the same way as the rest, then turn over the whole pack, so it is face down. Bring the cards into view. They have been out of sight for only a moment, and everyone believes it was just a swift gag.

'But I'm a first-rate operator,' you say, 'so I use real magic.' Put the pack face-down on the table, and prepare to spread the cards in a long ribbon. 'What was the name of your card?' you ask. As soon as the card is named, spread the

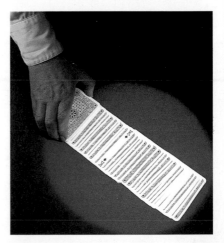

3

pack **(Fig. 3)**, and reveal the chosen card, now amazingly face upwards in the spread.

CARD SHARP

THE EFFECT

You mix the cards to a spectator's instructions, but they end up the same as they were at the start. The first time you do this trick it will probably fool you, too!

THE METHOD

Take all thirteen cards of one suit and lay them in numerical order on the table (Fig. 1). Tell a spectator to note the strict order of the cards, then square up the pile and turn it face down in your left hand.

❖❖❖❖❖❖❖❖❖❖❖

'We want to make sure the cards are thoroughly mixed,' you say, 'so you will tell me how to deal them.'

Explain that when the spectator says 'Deal', you will put a card on the table **(Fig. 2)**. When he or she says 'Dip', you will take the second card from the pile and put it on top of the first card **(Fig. 3)**, then deal both cards together on to the table.

You proceed to deal all the cards into a pile on the table, following the spectator's instructions to

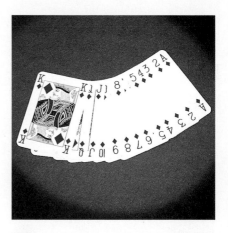

1

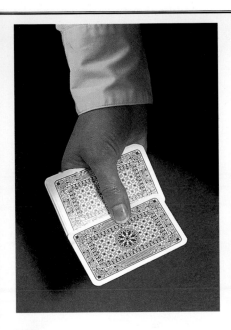

instructed. When all are dealt, pick up the pile and say:

'The truth is, whatever you tell me to do, the cards always go where I tell them to go.'

Turn over the cards and spread them in a line.

2

'Deal' or 'Dip' until all the cards are dealt. Now pick up the pile and square it.

'That has upset the order of the cards,' you say, 'but to upset them even further, we will go through the procedure once again.'

Once more you deal out the cards, carefully 'Dealing' or 'Dipping' as

3

Sure enough, all thirteen are back in numerical order, just as they were at the start.

X-RAY VISION

THE EFFECT

A spectator cuts a pack of cards into three face-down piles on the table. You gaze at the cards for a moment, then one by one you correctly name the top cards of the three piles.

THE METHOD

Before you start you must know the name of the top card on the pack. This is not difficult, just glimpse the card as you spread the pack, casually showing that it is ordinary (Fig. 1).

❖❖❖❖❖❖❖❖❖❖❖

1

known card on top **(Fig. 2)**. Let's say it's the Ten of Spades. You announce that you have X-ray vision. 'I've got enough to let me see through paper and other materials to a depth of about a millimetre. That's just deep

Put the pack face down on the table and ask a spectator to cut it into three roughly equal piles, keeping the cards face down. As this is being done, you must keep track of the pile with your

2

3

enough to read the identity of a playing card.' Pause, then add, 'Sometimes.'

You point to one of the piles, not the one with the known card on top, frown for a second, then say, 'That card is the Ten of Spades.'

Pick up the card, without revealing its face **(Fig. 3)**, and smile, as if you were right. We will assume this card is the Three of Diamonds.

Then point to the other pile with an unknown card on top and say, 'That's the Three of Diamonds.'

Pick up the card as before (it's the King of Hearts, say), smile as you square it against the other card you hold, and point to the remaining pile. This one has the remembered Ten of Spades on top. 'And that,' you say, 'is the King of Hearts.' Pick up the card, smile again, and add it to the other two.

You put the cards on the table one at a time, face up, naming each one as you do **(Fig. 4)**. The effect

4

is direct and impressive. You have accurately revealed the names of three playing cards without being able to see their faces.

STOP WHEN YOU LIKE

THE EFFECT

A spectator deals cards until he or she wants to stop. The last card dealt is turned over, and revealed to be the card identified in a note to the spectator.

THE METHOD

Before you begin, write 'You Will Stop At The Four Of Spades' on a piece of paper and place this inside a wallet. Put the wallet and the Four of Spades in your pocket.

Ask the spectator to shuffle the cards. 'Now deal them,' you say, 'and stop when you want.'

As you say this, indicate that the cards can be dropped anywhere on the table top – an over-tidy pile is the last thing you want.

While the cards are being dealt, take out the wallet, with the card face-down underneath it. Rehearse this so that you can do it without fumbling. When the dealing stops, drop the wallet on to the pile of cards **(Fig. 1)**, thus adding the Four of Spades to the pile.

1

'Look inside the wallet,' you say. The spectator reads the note inside. You move the wallet and turn over the top card on the pile, showing the message is correct.

2

TRICKS WITH GIMMICKED CARDS

THE FIVE TRICKS WHICH FOLLOW USE SPECIAL CARDS,

EASILY MADE, TO ENABLE YOU TO PERFORM CLOSE-UP

MAGIC IN THE PROFESSIONAL CLASS.

WHILE NO SLEIGHT-OF-HAND IS REQUIRED,

THESE ARE EFFECTS WHICH CREATE THE

IMPRESSION OF ADVANCED

CARD-HANDLING SKILL.

ODD DIVISION

THE METHOD

Cut a sheet of A4 paper into twenty or thirty squares. On all but one of them write the word 'Spades'. On the remaining one write 'Hearts'. Screw up the papers and drop them into a plastic bag; the one marked 'Hearts' goes in your pocket. You also need a dice, and a Three of Spades marked as shown (Fig. 1). This can be done using a water-resistant felt marker with a fine point.

16

1

To perform, say you have a card in your pocket which you placed there as the result of a premonition. 'It's the card that I knew someone would choose.'

Put the card face down on the table. Introduce the bag of folded papers. (Your own piece of paper is already tucked between the tips of your index and middle fingers).

'These pieces of paper all have suits written on then,' you say, reaching into the bag and apparently drawing one out. You bring out the one that was already

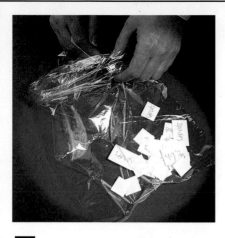

2

The spectator says that comes to three and a half.

'Really? Are you sure?' you say. Then you sigh. 'I thought it was weird, but who can argue with fate?'

Turn over the Three-and-a-half of Spades. The response to this mystifying trick should be gratifying. (The numbers on opposite sides of a dice, incidentally, always add up to seven.)

between your fingers **(Fig. 2)**. 'See, this says Hearts. Now somebody take one.'

A spectator draws Spades. 'That determines the card's suit,' you say. Show the dice. 'Now roll that, then add the number on top to the one on the bottom.'

The spectator rolls, say, a five **(Fig. 3)**. He adds five to the bottom number, which is two.

Now say, 'Divide the total by two and that will be the number of the card.'

3

THE ESTIMATE

THE EFFECT

You obtain an estimate of a card's position in the pack. The estimate seems unlikely, but it turns out to be right.

THE METHOD

Tear a quarter off a card. Place the card under five face-down cards (Fig. 1). Mark the upper left corner of the top card. Conceal the cards at the bottom of the pack.

To perform, spread the pack, being careful to keep the bottom cards bunched together to conceal the torn card. Ask a spectator to take a card **(Fig. 2)**. When he or she has done that, put the pack on the table.

Say, 'Remember your card, then put it face down on top of the pack.' The spectator complies. 'Now give the pack a complete cut, burying your card.' The

3

chosen card will now be directly under the torn card.

'I'm going to find your card by detecting its vibrations,' you announce, and begin to thumb through the face-down cards. When you see the card with the dot, cut it to the top so that the card and the cards beneath it move to the top **(Fig. 3)**. Then square the pack. Look confident as you turn over the marked card and say, 'Is this your card?' It isn't. You sigh and say you knew all along this wasn't the card: 'I just chose this one because it'll give me an estimate…'

Put the card to your ear. Listen and nod slowly. Put the card on the bottom of the pack and say, 'The estimate is four and three-quarters.'

Count the cards aloud, from the top of the pack. As you say, 'Four,' put down the fourth card and lift the mutilated one. **(Fig. 4)** '…And, er, three-quarters.'

4

Drop the torn card and pick up the next one. Ask the spectator to name the chosen card. Turn over the card in your hand and reveal that your earlier estimate was correct.

EDUCATED CARDS

THE EFFECT

You take turns with a spectator at laying cards on the table. You put down a card which bears the prophetic message 'You've Run Out Of Cards'.

THE METHOD

Make the message card by sticking a label across the face of another card. (Fig. 1). Place this card at the twenty-first position from the top of the face-down pack.

1

To perform, ask a spectator to cut some cards from the top of the pack, which is on the table, and put them in his or her pocket.

'Not too many,' you tell them, 'or we'll be here all night…' This ensures that fewer than twenty-one cards are taken! 'And now I'll have some.'

You must take twenty-one cards, and reverse their order. To do this, pick up the pack and deal twenty-one cards on to the table, one on top of the other **(Fig. 2)**; don't make it obvious that you are

2

3

counting. Put the pack aside and pick up your twenty-one cards.

'Right,' you say, 'now we'll deal cards on the table alternately. Me first.'

You deal a card, turning it face up as you do, then the spectator takes one from his or her pocket and deals it **(Fig. 3)**. Continue until you deal the message card. The spectator reaches in his or her pocket and finds that all the cards have gone **(Fig. 4)**.

As you'll discover, this trick is

entirely automatic, but it gives the impression of considerable skill on the part of the perfomer.

4

THE VANISHING QUEEN

THE METHOD

Prepare a Queen of Hearts by making two windows where the hearts were (Fig. 1). (You may need to use a scalpel to make the cut-out holes convincing enough to fool an onlooker.) This is your gimmick. Now lay the Fours from the pack in a face-up pile, with the Four of Hearts on top. Drop the gimmick on top. The face card looks like a Queen of Hearts. Put this set-up in your pocket.

1

To perform, bring out the cards, displaying the apparent Queen of Hearts on the top. Turn your hand over, so the backs of the cards are uppermost, and reach underneath with your forefinger. You seem to pull out the face card (supposedly the Queen of Hearts); in fact, you put your finger in the window opening of the gimmick and slide out the second card, the Four of Hearts. Put this on the table face down.

Repeat the above with the second and third 'Queens', really laying Fours on the table. Be careful to

2

'Watch these three, too,' you add, indicating the cards on the table.

Now ask if anyone remembers the suit of the Queen sticking out of your pocket. Whatever they say, pull it out and show that it is a Four. Ask a spectator to turn over the face-down cards on the table. They are all Fours.

Applause.

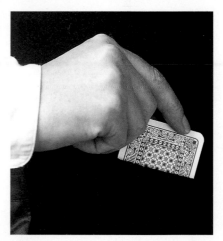

3

hold the cards so the thumb and little finger conceal the index marks on the gimmick **(Fig. 2)**.

You show the final Queen, which is really the gimmick with a Four behind. Put this pair in your pocket, letting the back of the Four stay in view. The gimmick drops down into the pocket.

'Watch this Queen,' you say, pointing to the protruding card **(Fig. 3)**.

CHATTY JOKER

THE METHOD

You need two identical Jokers. Cut one in half and write your message on the other. Put the Joker with the message face up on top of the pack. Put the half Joker over it and hold them together with an elastic band around the middle (Fig. 1); thus the half Joker will be held in place and its missing bottom concealed. On the face of it, the top card is a complete Joker.

To perform, drop the pack of cards on the table, drawing attention to the Joker: 'That's a very clever card,' you say. 'It can always get its message across.'

Pick up the cards and start to pull out the Joker from under the elastic band, grasping it at the lower end – that is, you are taking out the complete Joker. As you do so, turn the packet over so that it is face down by the time you draw the Joker out. Put the Joker face down on the table. Drop the cards into your pocket. In the same move, take out your pen and lay it

1

a short distance from the card. Tell a spectator to put one hand on the pen and the other on the card. 'Now,' you say, 'close your eyes and count to three.' Then tell the spectator to turn the card. The message will be there for all to see.

3

MIND-READING
WITH CARDS

PLAYING CARDS HAVE ALWAYS BEEN ASSOCIATED
WITH MIND-READING. IN THIS SECTION YOU LEARN
TO PERFORM TRICKS WHICH HAVE ALL THE MYSTERY
AND APPEAL OF AUTHENTIC PARANORMAL
DEMONSTRATIONS – AND THEY ARE A LOT
EASIER THAN THEY LOOK.

IMPOSSIBLE ODDS

THE METHOD

You will need all the black cards from the pack, plus one red card, which you place at the thirteenth position from the top. Do not let anyone know how your twenty-seven-card stack is made up. Put an elastic band around the cards and keep them in your pocket. You will also need to prepare a prediction (Fig. 1).

❖❖❖❖❖❖❖❖❖

You will choose a Red Card.

1

corresponding to the hour. The spectator keeps the cards he or she has counted off and hands back the remaining cards to you.

To perform, put the folded prediction on the table. Ask a spectator to imagine a clock, and imagine it chiming an hour. He or she is to put their cards behind their back and count off cards from the top of the pile

2

3

You now lay out the cards in the form of a clock face **(Fig. 2)**, starting at the 12 o'clock position and working anti-clockwise to 1 o'clock.

Ask the spectator what hour they chose. Count round to that position from the 12 o'clock card, and ask the spectator to turn over the card. It will be the red card **(Fig. 3)**. Ask another spectator to read out the prediction: 'You Will Choose A Red Card'.

Not exactly a shattering revelation. You ask the first spectator to look at the cards he or she still holds. 'They're all black, aren't they?' you ask.

The spectator agrees. You now turn over the few cards remaining after you finished making the clock face. 'These are black too, yes?' you say.

Finally, one by one, you turn over the rest of the clock cards, showing that they, too, are all black **(Fig. 4)**.

'There was only one red card,' you say. 'You chose it, and I predicted you would.'

4

MENTAL GUIDANCE

THE EFFECT

A spectator picks a card. Without looking, he pushes another card into the pack right beside his selection. You locate the spectator's selection. How?

THE METHOD

Tell the spectator to take half the pack, give you the rest and put their half behind their back. He or she takes out any card, looks at it, then puts it on top of their pack.

❖❖❖❖❖❖❖❖❖❖

'I'll show you first,' you say. Put your half behind your back; turn the second card face-upwards **(Fig. 1)**. Do this by lifting two cards with the right hand, pulling

the second card down with with the left thumb and flipping it over before the other card is dropped on top. This takes less than a

3

this: push the top card into the pack near the bottom; push the bottom card in near the top; then turn the top card face up and push it in anywhere near the centre **(Fig. 3)**. 'As you push this one in,' you say, 'I will send you mental guidance.'

NOTE: The insertion of top and bottom cards is a red herring. It gets the spectator accustomed to the manoeuvre – and it brings the turned-over card to the top!

The big finish. Spread the cards, showing there is one face-up near the centre, as expected **(Fig. 4)**. But beneath it is the card chosen by the spectator, located through your mental guidance.

second and should happen as the cards are being put behind your back. Now slip off the bottom card and bring it into view **(Fig. 2)**, to demonstrate that you have chosen a card. Put the card behind you again, but put it *face up* on the bottom of your pack, which you bring to the front.

'Now do as I showed you,' you say. When this has been done, the spectator brings his or her cards to the front and you put yours on top. 'Now your card is buried,' you say.

Tell the spectator to put the whole pack behind them and do

4

ASTOUNDING!

THE EFFECT

You predict the identity of a card freely-chosen under seemingly impossible conditions.

THE METHOD

Any Ace and any Four must be removed from the pack and set aside. Do this openly, keeping the cards face down, explaining that they are your prediction cards.

To perform, hand the pack to a spectator to shuffle, and ask him or her to think of a number between one and ten, which they must keep to themselves. Now tell the spectator to put the pack under the table and remove the number of cards that corresponds to their chosen number – i.e., if their number is four, they remove four cards **(Fig. 1)**. The spectator must put those cards in his pocket and hand back the pack.

'Now I'm going to start counting the pack,' you say, 'and when I get to the number you're thinking of, I want you to memorize it.' You

1

count the cards off the top of the pack, calling the number of each as you show its face, reversing the

2

order as you put them down **(Fig. 2)**.

Count this way until you reach number ten; count one more, saying 'Eleven', then ask if the spectator has remembered his or her card. As you say this, show and deal two more cards, without calling out numbers. This action is

3

never questioned. You have dealt thirteen cards in total. Put the dealt cards on top of the pack, and almost as an after-thought hold out the pack and tell the spectator to put back the cards they took off **(Fig. 3)**. The spectator's chosen card is fourteenth from the top. This is automatic. Show the Ace and Four you removed at the start.

4

'Fourteen,' you say. 'That is my prediction.'

Tell the spectator to count down to the fourteenth card **(Fig. 4)** and put it on the table, face down. When that is done, ask for the name of his card. Pause, then turn over the card on the table. Astounding!

THREE TIMES RIGHT

THE EFFECT

A number, a colour and a playing card are all successfully predicted by the performer.

THE METHOD

This employs the one-ahead principle, used in X-Ray Vision (page 12). You need a notepad, a pen, and a pack of cards with a known card on top – say the King of Clubs.

❖❖❖❖❖❖❖❖❖❖

1

To perform, tell your audience you will make a triple prediction.

Produce the notepad and the pen. Put the cards on the table.

Ask a spectator to think of a colour. Look pensive, then seem to be writing a colour on the pad. Actually, you write 'King of Clubs' – but don't let anyone see **(Fig. 1)**. Tear off the sheet and fold it twice. Now ask the spectator to name the colour – e.g., yellow.

Ask another spectator to take a banknote from his pocket and note the last three registration digits. On the pad write 'Yellow'. Fold the paper twice and drop it

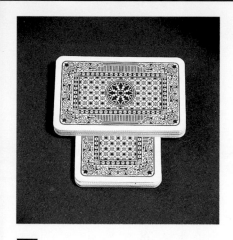

2

next to the first one. The spectator now names the digits – say, 246.

Tell a third spectator to cut the cards and put the cut cards beside the rest of the pack. Immediately, pick up the lower half of the pack. 'We'll mark the cut,' you say, as you lay this part across the top of the other, making a cross shape **(Fig. 2)**. The King of Clubs is now on top of the lower part of the pack.

Now you write 246. Fold the paper and drop it on top the other two papers. Lift the top part of the

pack and take off the card under the cut.

Say, 'Let's see your card.' Show it is the King of Clubs **(Fig. 3)**.

Now pick up and open the pieces of paper. Ask the first spectator to name the chosen colour; put the paper with 'Yellow' written on it face up on the table. Do the same with the numbers and, for your finale, the name of the playing card.

3

PRECOGNITION

THE EFFECT

Put a sealed envelope containing your precognition on the table. A spectator chooses a card, and is asked to open the envelope. Inside is a duplicate of their chosen card.

THE METHOD

To prepare, put a duplicate of the 'force' card (here the Eight of Hearts) in an envelope. The Eight of Hearts in your pack should be the tenth card from the top of the pack.

❖❖❖❖❖❖❖❖❖❖❖

To perform, tell a spectator that you will persuade him or her to choose a card according to the laws of numerology, but that the numbers will be of his or her own choosing. Hand over the pack and ask for a number between ten and twenty. (The trick won't work with twenty!) Let's assume they pick sixteen. Tell them to deal sixteen cards on to the table.

1

'Now put the rest of the pack aside and add together the digits of your chosen number,' you say. The number was sixteen; 1 + 6 = 7. Tell the spectator to pick up the

sixteen cards and count down to the seventh. This card should be turned face up **(Fig. 1)**. The card in the envelope will be identical to the one chosen by the spectator.

4

KEY CARDS

All the tricks in this section use the 'key card' principle. The key card is a card which is known to the performer and lies at a certain position in the pack. Sometimes it is gimmicked, sometimes not. In the interests of variety, several different key cards will be described.

THE BUCKLE

THE EFFECT

**You find a selected card
while holding the pack
behind your back.**

THE METHOD

**Spread out the pack, face
down, and ask for a card
to be chosen. As the
spectator looks at the card,
close the pack and buckle it
upwards (Fig. 1).**

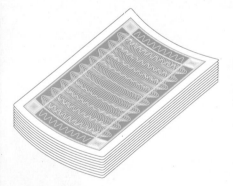

pack to the spectator for shuffling.

The chosen card is now the only flat card, which means the pack is markedly divided at the place where the card is inserted; the card automatically becomes the key **(Fig. 2)**.

Take back the cards and square them. You will be able to see the break. If the chosen card is close to the top or bottom of the pack, make a cut to put it nearer the centre. If the card is right on the top or bottom of the pack, leave it where it is.

1

Spread the cards again and let the spectator put back his or her card anywhere they like. Hand the

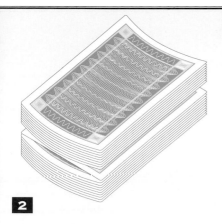

2

Put the cards behind your back, saying you will find the selected card by feeling its emanations.

With the pack behind your back, hold the cards lightly with the right thumb on one long edge and the right fingers on the other (**Fig 3**). Now gently cut the cards and you will feel them break naturally. The chosen card, which is now wider than the others, will be the bottom card of the upper part of the cut. Slide it out into your right hand (**Fig. 4**) and put the rest of the cards in your left hand.

Smile as you bring out the pack and put it down.

Widen your smile as you bring forward the chosen card and put it face up on the table.

3

4

KEEP THINKING

THE METHOD

Invite a spectator to shuffle a pack of cards. Take back the cards and spread them face down. Ask the spectator to pick one and look at it. Square the pack. Tell the spectator to put the card back. Lift off half the pack with your right hand, extending your left hand for the return of the card. As you do, glance at the bottom card in your right hand (Fig. 1). This is your key card.

1

As soon as the spectator's card is returned, drop the cards from your right hand on top of it. Hand him the complete pack, telling him to shuffle it.

NOTE: As long as the cards are shuffled in the normal overhand fashion, the key card and the chosen card will stay together, no matter how much the pack is shuffled and cut.

Take back the pack and turn it face up. Start running the cards between your hands, looking for the key card **(Fig. 2)**.

As you do this, tell the spectator to keep thinking of his card. 'Keep thinking,' you say, 'Keep thinking…'

thinking Three of Diamonds, Three of Diamonds, Three of Diamonds…', until the spectator realizes you are staring at him.

Then, you say 'Your chosen card is the Three of Diamonds.'

And, of course, it is.

2

3

As soon as you see the key card, you know the card on its right is the chosen card **(Fig. 3).** 'Keep thinking,' you murmur, 'Keep thinking.' Go past the chosen card, still murmuring, 'Keep

CUTTING CORNERS

THE METHOD

To make the key card, shorten the upper left and lower right corners of a face-down card with nail clippers, or a pair of scissors (Fig. 1). Now put the card in the pack.

No matter which way the face-down cards are turned, the key card will have a short corner at the outer left corner of the pack.

To learn the technique of using this card, bury it in the pack and run your thumb down the outer left corner (Fig. 2); as the key card passes, you will hear – and feel – a click, caused by the short

1

2

3

card and the card above it passing as one.

To stop at the key card, run your thumb once down the cards to get a rough idea where the key card is located, then do it again, trying to stop at the exact spot. This will happen automatically as you gain experience – this technique is called 'riffling'.

To use the key, have it on the bottom of the pack as you spread the cards and ask for one card to be taken **(Fig. 3)**. Put the pack on the table, tell the spectator to return the chosen card to the top, then ask him or her to cut the

pack as many times as they wish. (The first cut ensures that the key is positioned on top of the chosen card.) Now ask another spectator to shuffle the cards.

Finally take back the pack and riffle to locate the key card. Give the pack a complete cut at that point. The key goes to the bottom and the chosen card is on top **(Fig. 4)**.

Ask the spectator to name the chosen card, then drop the top card face up on the table as you say, 'You can cut and shuffle all you like, but I always find the card I'm after.'

4

MOVING FINGER

THE EFFECT

A spectator makes you find his card – even though he has no idea where it is.

THE METHOD

Your key is the top card of the pack. It is not gimmicked, but on its back you have marked diagonally opposite corners with a pencil dot (Fig. 1).

1

Ask for a card to be selected, then cut the pack with your right hand. Offer the lower half for the return of the card.

The cards in your right hand are turned over ready for an overhand shuffle and the key card (top) is drawn on to the lower pile **(Figs. 2 and 3)**. Continue to shuffle the other cards on top. This looks perfectly fair, but of course the key card is now on top of the chosen card. When you have shuffled off all the cards, give the pack a couple of cuts then spread it face down in a ribbon across the table, noting the position of the key card.

2

3

Ask the spectator to hold your wrist, then extend your arm over the cards at a height of about 50 cm (20 in), your finger pointing down **(Fig. 4)**.

'You don't know where your card is,' you say. 'Neither do I. But concentrate on its name.'

Begin above one end of the ribbon and let the spectator draw your hand slowly along. You know the card with the dot (the key) is on the right of the chosen card. When you are almost above the key, start to bring your hand down. To the audience, your hand is being guided.

Let your finger come to rest on the card to the left of the key. Slide it out with your fingertips.

'Name your card,' you say.

The spectator names it. Turn over the card. You have performed a miracle.

4

BLIND FAITH

THE METHOD

The key card in this trick is a wide card, made by glueing together two cards slightly out of register so that the finished product is a card a fraction wider (and longer) than the others in the pack. Wherever this card lies in the pack, it can be easily located by touch. More importantly, it can also be used to mark the point at which the pack will be cut.

To perform, have the key on the bottom as you spread the cards and ask for one to be chosen. Tell the spectator to put his or her selection back on top. Make a complete cut, putting the key on top of the chosen card. Ask the spectator to shuffle the pack. Then, take back the pack and square it. You will be able to feel the key card. If it is near the top or bottom, make a couple of cuts, openly. The idea is to get the card near the middle, where it is easier to cut. Put the pack on the table.

Say, 'You've done all you can to lose that card of yours. But I have

1

total faith in my ability to find it.'

Without looking, cut it at the wide card, leaving the chosen card on top of the pack **(Fig. 1)**. Ask for the name of the chosen card. Still without looking, turn over the top card and throw it down, face up.

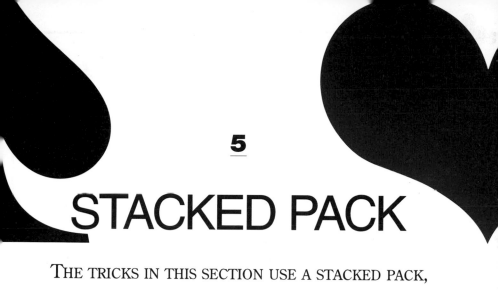

5

STACKED PACK

THE TRICKS IN THIS SECTION USE A STACKED PACK,
WHICH IS A PACK OF CARDS ARRANGED SO THAT YOU CAN
PERFORM ASTONISHING CARD TRICKS VERY EASILY.
THE STACK USED HERE IS THE ONE DEVISED BY
SI STEBBINS, AND IS EXPLAINED AT THE
BEGINNING OF THE FIRST TRICK.

BLINDFOLD MIND PROBE

THE EFFECT

You are blindfolded. A card is selected as usual. Without asking any questions, you correctly name the card.

THE METHOD

Arrange the cards so they run in the order Ace, 4, 7, 10, King, 3, 6, 9, Queen, 2, 5, 8, Jack, and in the repeating order of Clubs, Hearts, Spades, Diamonds (Fig. 1).

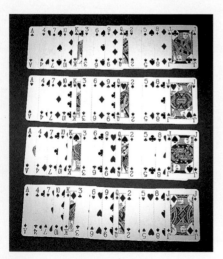

1

Each card is three higher than the one before – e.g., if you cut a Two, the card beneath it will be a Five; cut a Nine and the next card will be twelve (a Queen). The suit order – Clubs, Hearts, Spades, Diamonds – is remembered by picturing the word CHaSeD. If you cut the Three of Hearts, the next card is the Six of Spades.

To perform the trick blindfold, have the stacked pack ready in your hands; it can be cut as often as you wish without disturbing the stack. Ask a spectator to blindfold you with a large handkerchief, which you adjust 'for comfort', with your thumbs, so you can see clearly down either side of your nose.

Spread the cards face down between your hands and ask for one to be chosen **(Fig. 2)**. As it is taken, cut the pack at that point and put the bottom portion on top. Turn the pack face up for a moment as you square it and you will see the bottom card **(Fig. 3)** – let's say it's the Seven of Clubs.

Put down the cards. Ask the spectator to concentrate on his card.

3

The bottom card of the pack was originally above the selected card; it's a Seven, so the chosen card must be a Ten – and it is a Club, so the chosen card must be a Heart. The Ten of Hearts.

'I'm getting an impression,' you say, as soon as you have made the simple calculation. Slowly name the card.

2

THOUGHT PROCESS

THE EFFECT

The selections of two spectators are divined before they themselves know what cards they have chosen.

THE METHOD

You will need two stacked packs. Put one pack in front of one spectator, hand another spectator the second pack and tell him or her to put it behind their back.

48

Address the first spectator. 'Cut that pack as many times as you want, complete cuts, putting the top half underneath each time.' When that is done, say, 'Take off the top card, don't look at it, and put it in your pocket. Now take the next card, no looking, and sit on it. Put the pack on the table.'

Turn to the second spectator. 'Cut the pack behind your back, then take off the top card, turn it face up, and slip it into the middle of the face-down pack.' **(Fig. 1)**

Turn to the first spectator again.

1

'I'm going to repeat your actions,' you say, 'and try to make my

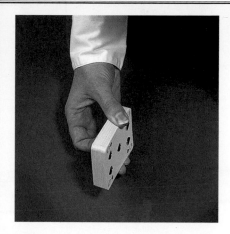

2

thought process recover the image of what you did.'

Pick up the pack and glimpse the bottom card (e.g. the Five of Spades) **(Fig. 2)**. Now mime the action of taking a card from the top and pocketing it, then taking a second card and sitting on it.

'Now I'll look,' you say. Take the invisible card from your pocket and name it: 'The Eight of Diamonds' (the card after the Five of Spades). Ask the spectator to remove the card from his pocket. It matches!

Go through the same manoeuvre with the invisible card you sat on; stare at it, then say, 'the Jack of Clubs' (the card after the Eight of Diamonds). Ask the spectator to reveal his sat upon card. Again, a match! Turn to the second spectator and say, 'Put the pack face up on the table.'

He or she does this **(Fig. 3)**. You see which card is on top of the pack (e.g. the Ace of Clubs). You do a quick calculation, then announce, 'The card you reversed in the pack is the Four of Hearts.'

Spread the pack, find the face-down card, and turn it over – the Four of Hearts. You are a legend.

3

INTERLOPER

THE EFFECT

While you are out of the room, a card is freely chosen from the pack, then put back. You return, look through the cards and name the one that was chosen.

THE METHOD

The pack is stacked. Ask a spectator to cut it as many times as he or she likes. When this has been done, square it up and put it in the middle of the table.

'I'm leaving the room,' you say. 'While I'm out, I want you to reach into the pack and take out a card. Show it to everyone, then put it back on top and cut it into the pack. When you've done that, call me in again.' When you return to the room, pick up the cards and turn them face up. Spread them between your hands (**Fig. 1**), saying, 'In the last couple of minutes, one card of these fifty-two has suffered a little more disturbance than the others. I should be able to sense its stress as it passes through my fingers.'

The place where the card is inserted, however, will have a card which is out of sequence **(Fig. 3).** (In the picture the odd card is the Seven of Hearts.)

When you find the card, pull it out.

'I was right,' you say. 'This is a very badly stressed card.'

Turn it around and show its face. 'Poor thing.'

2

Start to go through the cards, taking your time. You note only the suits. The sequence of Clubs, Hearts, Spades, Diamonds is repeated over and over, all the way through the pack, except at the place where a card was removed, and at the place where it was replaced.

You will know where it was taken from, because there will simply be a gap in the sequence **(Fig. 2).**

3

SUPER SPELLER

THE EFFECT

This trick appears to be a
self-fulfilling prophecy. The
look-alike of a chosen card
is found by spelling out
seven words.

THE METHOD

Spread the stacked cards
between your hands to have
one chosen. Make the spread
wide, emphasizing the
freedom of choice (Fig. 1).

1

When the card is taken, break the
pack at that point and put the
cards from underneath on top.
Now address the spectator.

'You took that card for me – that is
my card. I want you to look at it
and picture its look-alike. What I
mean is, if you picked the Ace of
Hearts, its look-alike would be the
Ace of Diamonds, because it has
the same colour and the same
number. The look-alike is your
card.'

Make sure that is clear, then
continue. 'I don't know what card

2

Start to spell the words you have just spoken (twenty-six letters), putting down a card for each letter. When you have put down the card for the last letter of 'card', pause as you did when you spoke the phrase, then spell out the word 'easily'.

On the final letter, hold the card face down **(Fig. 3)**. Tell the spectator to turn over the card on the table. Now reveal the one you hold. It is the look-alike – the spectator's card.

you picked, neither does anybody else. Put it face down on the table in front of you, and keep thinking of its look-alike – your card.'

Pick up the pack and glimpse the bottom card – say the Six of Hearts **(Fig. 2)**. That means the spectator has the Nine of Spades. Believe it or not, the look-alike of this card, which is the Nine of Clubs, is halfway down the pack, at number twenty-six from the top.

'Now I will find your card,' you say. Pause, then add, 'easily.'

3

GROUP REVELATION

THE EFFECT

Freely chosen cards are distributed among spectators. One by one, you reveal each of their selections.

THE METHOD

The stacked pack is spread face down as you approach a spectator. 'Pull out a bunch of cards,' you say. 'Keep one for yourself and hand out the rest to other spectators.'

When the cards have been removed, cut the pack at that point, putting the lower part on top. Square the cards, glimpsing the bottom card. Let's say the spectator took six cards, and the card you glimpsed was the King of Diamonds **(Fig. 1)**. Now pretend you are gaining an impression of a dark card. Of course you start with the card which would have followed the King of Diamonds – the Three of Clubs. Name the card and ask if anyone has it. When it is returned, put it at the bottom of the pack. Do the same with each successive card you reveal.

1

As you proceed with the revelations, you will find that people react in a way that shows you are about to name their card. Use these clues to home in on individuals. This will reinforce the idea that you're receiving 'spirit' messages!

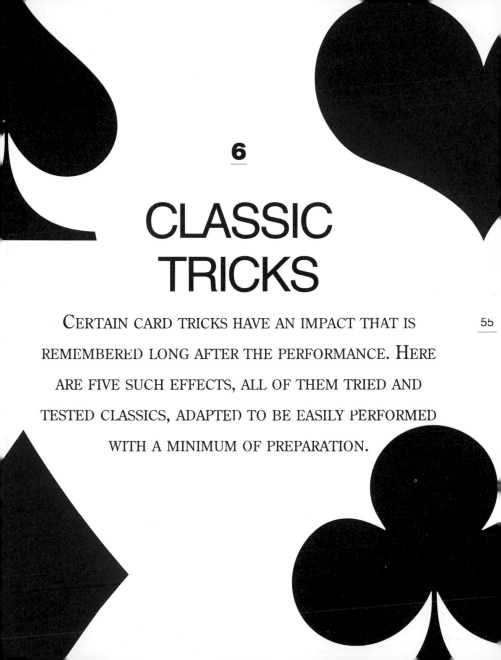

6

CLASSIC
TRICKS

CERTAIN CARD TRICKS HAVE AN IMPACT THAT IS
REMEMBERED LONG AFTER THE PERFORMANCE. HERE
ARE FIVE SUCH EFFECTS, ALL OF THEM TRIED AND
TESTED CLASSICS, ADAPTED TO BE EASILY PERFORMED
WITH A MINIMUM OF PREPARATION.

SURPRISE ACES

THE EFFECT

A trick appears to go wrong, then it goes right, and then there's an unexpected four-Ace finish. Tricks with Aces are always popular, which is why there are two in this section!

THE METHOD

In this stack the Aces are at the bottom; on top of them is a face-up Five. This set-up enables easy overhand shuffling. The bottom five cards must not disturbed.

1

To perform the trick, spread the face-down pack between your hands, making sure the lower cards are bunched to hide the fact that one is face up **(Fig. 1)**. Ask a spectator to select a card and remember it. Square the pack and put it on the table.

Ask the spectator to put the chosen card on top of the pack, then to lose it by cutting the pack and completing the cut. The chosen card will now be somewhere near the centre of the pack, directly under the stack of four Aces.

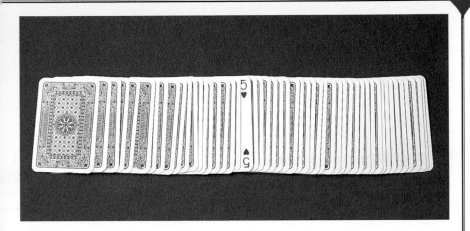

2

Spread the pack in a ribbon across the table and smile confidently as you point to the face-up card **(Fig. 2)**. The spectator will not hesitate to say that isn't his or her card.

'I know,' you tell them, pushing out the card from the spread. 'But this card tells me where your card is.' Now you count to five, pushing out a card for each number (the four Aces, plus one) **(Fig. 3)**. Ask for the name of the spectator's selection and turn over the fifth card. It's the spectator's card.

'So I found it after all,' you say.

Turn over the four Aces one by one. 'And it seems that's not all I've found.'

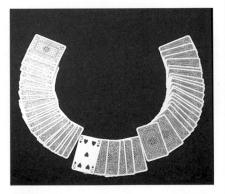

3

CUTTING THE ACES

THE EFFECT

Magicians often demonstrate their skill by cutting the Aces; in this version, a spectator emulates this without knowing how it was done!

THE METHOD

A fresh pack of cards is prepared by putting the four Aces on top of the pack. The trick is to keep your eye on the pile with the four Aces on top.

1

Put the cards on the table and ask a spectator to cut them into four roughly equal piles **(Fig. 1)**. Say, 'I want you to mix the top cards in the following way.' Point at a pile (not the one with the Aces), tell the spectator to pick it up, transfer three cards from the top to the bottom of the pile, then put one card on the top of each of the three piles on the table **(Fig. 2)**. The spectator must now put down

2

pile is picked up and the transferring is carried out for the last time. When the fourth pile is back on the table, ask if the spectator knows what has happened. The answer will probably be 'no'. 'Well,' you say, 'if my guess is correct, it's something pretty spectacular ...' Turn over the top cards one by one **(Fig. 3)**, and show how clever spectators can be when they do as they're told.

3

the stack he or she is holding and repeat the actions with the other three piles. Point to the piles in turn, being careful to point last to the pile with the four Aces.

By the time the fourth pile is picked up, the procedure of transferring cards from other piles will have put three extra cards on top of the Aces. These will go to the bottom of the pile when the Ace

SENSE OF TOUCH

THE EFFECT

The performer finds a selected card using only his sense of touch.

THE METHOD

The cards are shuffled and a spectator is asked to think of a number between one and twenty. The spectator memorizes the card which lies at his chosen number from the top.

1

Now take the pack from him or her and say this: 'Only you know the number and the card. Even so, I can find the card by sense of touch alone.'

Put the pack behind your back. Take off the bottom card and put it on top of the pack. Peel off the new bottom card and bring it forward, back outwards.

'I think I have found your card,' you say, and slip it into your pocket.

Bring the pack forward again. 'If I'm wrong, then your card will still

60

be at your number. What's the number?'

Suppose he says ten. Count cards off the top of the pack one at a time, face down. When you come to the tenth card, slide it across the table.

'If I'm wrong, that's your card.'

The next stage is not 'sleight of hand', but a straightforward move. As the spectator reaches for the card on the table, you lift the inner end of the next card (their chosen card!) with your thumb and let it drop back against your curled little finger, which now pushes the card into the curl of your opposite hand **(Figs. 1 and 2)**, where it stays **(Fig. 3)**.

The spectator turns over the card. It's not theirs. While this is happening, your hand is going into your pocket. Slide the card from your palm to your fingertips and bring it out. Ask the name of the spectator's card. Show that you were right.

2

3

COUNTDOWN

THE EFFECT

Although the performer never touches the cards, he knows exactly where a chosen card lies in the pack.

THE METHOD

From bottom to top, stack the Ace to Ten of any one suit (e.g. Diamonds) (Fig. 1). The cards are in this position when you put the pack, face down, in front of a spectator.

1

Now tell the spectator to look at the card removed from the pack. 'Put it back on top and give the pack a full cut, which will bury the card.'

When the card is buried, tell the

2

'From now on,' you say, 'I'm not going to touch the cards. I want you to spread the pack and slide out one card, then square up the pack again.'

between Ace and Ten shows, remember it – let's say it's the Three **(Fig. 3)**. Tell the spectator to turn the pack face down. 'Put a finger on the pack again and think of your card,' you say. 'I sense its position.… It's at number five from the top. Whoops! You moved! Now it's at number four … No, you moved again. Now it's at number three. Take a look. Quick, before it moves again!'

The spectator counts to number three (or whatever) and there, sure enough, is the chosen card **(Fig. 4)**.

63

spectator to turn the pack face up, rest a fingertip on the top card for a second **(Fig. 2)**, then give the pack another complete cut. What happens next will depend on how the pack is cut. As soon as the top card is a Diamond with a value anywhere between Ace and Ten, you know where the chosen card lies. For example, if the spectator cuts the Four of Diamonds to the top of the pack, then the chosen card will be at position number four when the pack is face down. If no Diamond card shows, ask the spectator to press a finger on the top card again (a red herring!) and cut once more. As soon as a Diamond

4

INSTANT SPELL

THE EFFECT

A spectator finds his own chosen card by spelling its name. Of all the methods of achieving this classic effect, this is the most direct.

THE METHOD

Put the Ten of Clubs, Six of Spades, Jack of Hearts, Eight of Spades, and Nine and Queen of Diamonds face down on the pack, then nine assorted cards on top.

To perform, start moving cards from the your left hand to your right, without reversing their order **(Fig. 1)**. As you reach the fifth or sixth card, say, 'Stop me when you like.' Speak a little impatiently – you will almost certainly be stopped on one of the set-up cards. (If you are not stopped on a set-up card, change tack; spot the bottom card of the pack and perform a 'key card' trick!)

Show the spectator the card he or she stopped at, and say, 'Look at this card and remember it.' Put the card back on the pack and drop all the right-hand cards on

top of it. The pack is now as it was at the start. Hand the cards to the spectator and ask them to spell the name of their card, starting from the top of the pack, including the word 'of'. The spectator's card will show up on the final letter 'S'.

1